INTRODUCTION BY DAVID HALBERSTAM

EDITED BY ROBERT HARSHORN SHIMSHAK

b11277786

suburbia *BILL OWENS*

fotofolio

It stands as one of the great migrations in American history. Starting in the years immediately after World War II, millions of ordinary Americans, flush with the disposable income saved up during the war, longing for more space and, above all, a better life for their kids, began to move to the suburbs. Led by an innovative builder named Bill Levitt who adapted the techniques of Henry Ford's mass-production assembly line from making cars to building houses (because houses were too large for an assembly line, Levitt shrewdly brought the assembly line *to* the location), there was nothing less than an explosion in middle-class housing. In 1944, there were only 114,000 new housing starts in the country; by 1950, as Levitt and his many imitators hit their stride, the figure was *1.7 million* new starts. Americans, after all, were now automobile-propelled as never before. They were on an unparalleled binge of car buying and new highways were springing up around all our great cities. What had once been a distant commute was now accessible. Where once on the outskirts of town there had been bucolic locations virtually devoid of human beings, miniature cities of 25,000–50,000 people sprouted up as if someone had quietly planted them during the night. Many a dairy farmer whose job it had been to provide milk for a neighboring city now found that his land was vastly more valuable than his cows, and was moved aside by the suburban explosion, which was like an irresistible force of nature. By 1980 some 60 million Americans had moved to the suburbs, while the population of most American cities had dropped considerably over a thirty-year period.

In a way, Bill Owens stumbled into this book. The migration was all around him—it was as if he was being swallowed up in it. Everywhere he turned, houses were springing up, row upon row; what had been farmland one day was a city the next. In 1968 he was breaking in as a photographer for a small newspaper in Livermore, California. And there, around him every day, was this new, stunning social phenomenon. And so he began photographing it—understanding that he was witnessing something special, that these people were, in the best American way buying not just houses, but dreams—often long suppressed in their families—of a better life.

When *Suburbia* first came out, it immediately became a small classic. Over the years it has reached cult status, and I am delighted to be part of its reintroduction to fans of Americana and serious admirers of exceptional photography. I think it succeeds for two main reasons. One is that Owens, in the best and most natural way, found himself a part of a major social movement and shrewdly understood that something *emotional* as well as physical was taking place around him. The second reason is that he did not—unlike all too many Americans of that period, particularly those with an artistic sensibility—condescend to the people who were part of the migration. Altogether too many social critics, themselves secure citizens of the middle class for several generations, mocked the new suburbs, particularly the outward uniformity of the homes, as if that uniformity reflected a spiritual uniformity inside. Instead Owens wisely respected the sense of liberation the suburbs represented to those arriving there. "I find a sense of freedom in the suburbs…," he quotes the head of one family. "You assume the mask of suburbia for outward appearances and yet no one knows what you really do." What comes through is Owens' empathy for the people he photographed.

For many of those in the migration, it was an adventure in changing class as well as changing address: the first venture, however tentative, into the great new American middle-class. Many were the children of people who had never owned a home and who had rented cold-water flats in the years before the war. As such, the suburban experience was more often than not an optimistic one. These were young Americans living better than their parents, enjoying a confidence about the quality of life that their parents had never been able to enjoy, and thinking now of sending their own children to college. Owens understood the people who were making this journey, sympathized with them, and caught what was perhaps the most important part of the entire migration—the optimism and belief that owning your own house and a small patch of land represented the first step to a better life and a higher level of personal freedom and dignity. What he has given us is a small, understated book about the hopes of ordinary people, which is why it is so special and why it still endures.

DAVID HALBERSTAM

Sunday afternoon we get it together. I cook the steaks and my wife makes the salad.

One of the joys of living in the suburbs is taking care of your own lawn.

I find a sense of freedom in the suburbs.... You assume the mask of suburbia for outward appearances and yet no one knows what you really do.

I bought the lawn in six-foot rolls. It's easy to handle. I prepare the ground and my wife and son helped roll out the grass. In one day you have a front yard.

11

We moved up to a nicer house. We thought we'd do better, but the real estate man got us. Closing costs were supposed to be $295 but they turned out to be $750. They have you where they want you—you've already moved into the house.

We're not doing too badly.

People throw away a lot of good things: clothes, toys, broken toasters, record players, and in the newer areas they throw out tables and chairs that don't fit in their new house. The ecology movement doesn't matter. I make over $250 in coke bottles. People here can't realize there are poor people in the world. They can't think about the needs of other people.

We had a ball on the Fourth of July. The whole neighborhood came out for the parade.

I enjoy cooking, dogs, cats, kids, soccer, and living here.

We lived in our house for a year without any living room furniture. We wanted to furnish the room with things we loved, not early attic or leftovers. Now we have everything but the pictures and the lamps.

Togetherness really exists in our family. My daughter and I operate the lunch room at the Valley Inn. My sons work part-time with their dad, hanging sheet-rock. And my eldest two sons work at the Gulf gas station on P St. We have seven cars and two motorcycles in our family.

I believe in women's liberation. I'm tired of the image of the woman who has the most sanitary toilet bowl, the cleanest floor, and the brattiest kids as the supermother. I want to be able to change with my children and to change with my life as I grow older. Staying at home and taking care of the kids doesn't help.

My husband, Pat, has a theory about watering our newly seeded lawn. The water has to trinkle from
heaven and fall like tender little rain drops...otherwise the lawn won't grow properly.

I get a lot of compliments on the front room wall. I like Italian Syrocco floral designs over the mantle. It goes well with the Palos Verde rock fireplace.

We've been married two months and everything we own is in this room.

This isn't what we really want—the tract house, the super car, etc....But as long as we are wound up in this high speed environment, we will probably never get out of it! We don't need the super car to be happy; we really want a small place in the country where you can breathe the air.

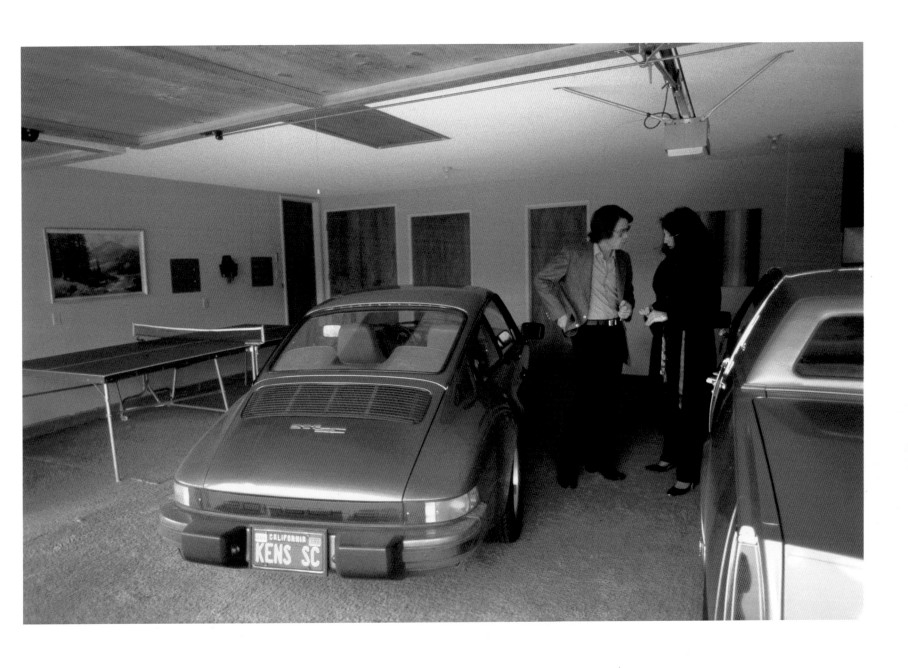

He's a typical Californian who doesn't know how to relax.

We're home three weekends a year. Our camper is our real home. Being a member of the National Campers and Hikers Association gives our family the opportunity and the enjoyment of getting out of town every weekend…and to camp with other camper families.

The California garage today, out of necessity, requires that you move the cars out and the tools in. To a point I enjoy working in the garage, but I'd rather be doing something else.

This is our outdoor garage sale…last minute kids' items for Christmas shoppers.

I find the tensions of the day go away when I run a few miles before dark. The light is different, I hear new things and smell new odors like a fireplace burning oakwood. Sometimes I find that dogs are not man's best friend.

We enjoy having these things.

Tuo-Tuo, our dog, is a very expensive household pet. It costs 30¢ a day to feed him—that's $109 a year—and $13 a month to have him groomed—that's $155 a year—not including the vet bill. We spend over $350 a year, but we don't care. We love him.

I'm OK You're OK is a study of transcendental meditation.

This is Valerie's world in miniature. She makes it what she wants it to be…without war, racial hate or misunderstanding. Ken and Barbie (dolls) are man and woman rather than Mom and Dad. They enjoy living and having a camper truck is the good life. Today Valerie has the chicken pox and can't go out and play.

I enjoy giving a Tupperware party in my home. It gives me a chance to talk to my friends. But really, Tupperware is a homemaker's dream, you save time and money because your food keeps longer.

It's a great pleasure to watch yourself make love in the six dozen mirrors that line the ceilings and walls. I've spent a tremendous amount of thought and planning to get the total effect of the bedroom. It's fascinating to watch our friends' reactions to seeing the luxury and sensuousness of the room. Our bedroom is the most enjoyable room in the house.

We feel most people have the wrong attitude towards sex, that it's nasty and to be done only in the dark. With us sex takes care of itself.

I put it off until I can't stand it anymore. The rottenest job in the whole house is cleaning the bathroom.

Doing laundry is death defying; as soon as you're done you have to start all over again.

I wanted Christina to learn some responsibility for cleaning her room, but it didn't work.

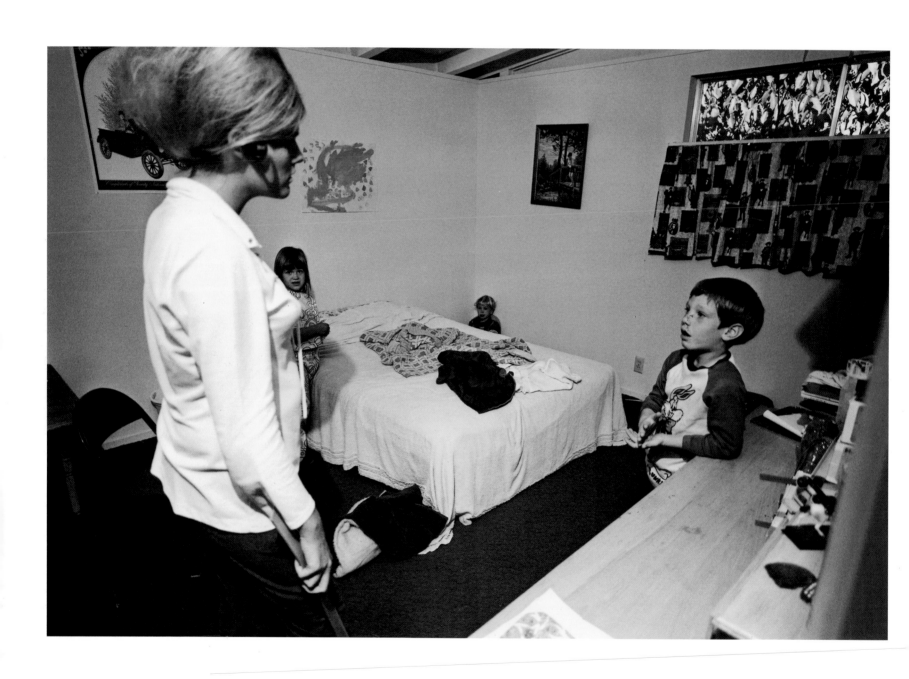

I believe in strict discipline of my children, but they also deserve the right of self-explanation. 46

Andrew doesn't like to go to the bathroom alone.

I don't like the space walk. It's Saturday morning and I want to see cartoons. 48

We'd rather play games than watch TV.

How can I worry about the damned dishes when there are children dying in Vietnam.

We're really happy. Our kids are healthy, we eat good food, and we have a really nice home.

I enjoy the suburbs. They provide Girl Scouts, PTA, Little League, and soccer for my kids. The thing I miss most is Black cultural identity for my family. White middle-class suburbia can't supply that. Here the biggest cultural happening has been the opening of two department stores.

I love to cook. Meal time is the only time the family is together. In spite of my modern kitchen, cooking dinner for six takes two hours. Then the kids inhale the food in minutes. After they are grown maybe they will remember the meals that their mother cooked.

Because we live in the suburbs we don't eat too much Chinese food. It's not available in the super-markets so on Saturday we eat hot dogs.

My hobby is drinking. On the weekends I enjoy getting together with my friends and boozing.

We really enjoy living in a mobile home. My hobby is collecting coins and my wife plays her Wurlitzer for entertainment.

We've been collecting rocks since 1958. It's enjoyable to get out into the open and hunt for rocks, and it's really fun to cut open a rock and find a gem inside.

I have all the cares of home ownership and the privacy of apartment living. We have an investment in the house. So I find myself doing all the undesirable chores to protect our investment.

Before the dissolution of our marriage my husband and I owned a bar. One day a toilet broke and we brought it home.

Monday, Tuesday, Wednesday, Thursday…and Friday I have my hair done.

We really enjoy getting together with our friends to drink and dance. It's a wild party and we're having a great time.

This is our second annual Fourth of July block party. This year thirty-three families came for beer, barbequed chicken, corn on the cob, potato salad, green salad, macaroni salad, and watermelon. After eating and drinking we staged our parade and fireworks.

If Bank of America knew the truth…

I bought the Doughboy pool for David and the kids and now no one wants to take the responsibility for cleaning it.

Hockney painted this pool.

Bourbon and Seven is my favorite drink.

We don't have to conform.

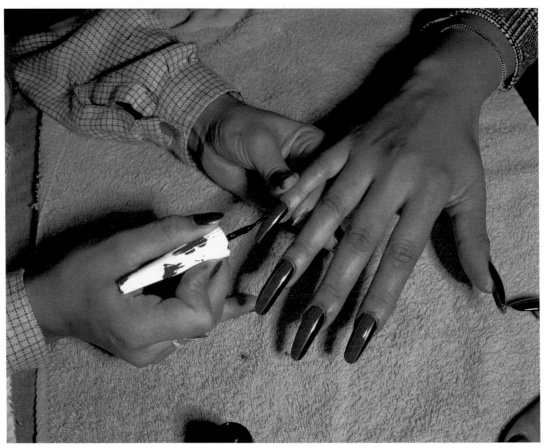

It costs $65.00 to have your nails done.

I put my hair up once or twice a week. It's the only way I can get curls in it. When it's combed out,

I'm willing to be seen in public.

Some days when there is no one to play with I build Glenn a tent play house out of two chairs and two blankets.

81

My kids love soccer and this is Saturday morning before the game.

I don't feel that Richie playing with guns will have a negative effect on his personality. (He already wants to be a policeman). His childhood gun-playing won't make him into a cop-shooter. By playing with guns he learns to socialize with other children. I find the neighbors who are offended by Richie's gun, either the father hunts or their kids are the first to take Richie's gun and go off and play with it.

The best way to help your city government and have fun is to come out on a Saturday morning and pull weeds in a median strip.

84

My dad thinks it's a good idea to take all the leaves off the tree and rake up the yard. I think he's crazy.

I believe organized sports make better citizens of children. I have four boys and they all play baseball and soccer. They learn to cooperate with others…and that winning isn't always the most important thing to do.

Bonnie and Bob Powers

Milton and Sylvia Grissom

Jane and Norm Volponi

Aaron and Myra Latkin

Paul Dumas and Linda McPherson

Judy and Walt Hanhy

Bruce and Pat Barney

Richard and Ivy Osyerude

Ann and Mel Lemos

Janet and Lee Keene

Celia and John Baker and John Jr.

Rhonda and Joy Gilbert

Sara and Abraham Goldberg

Renee and Dennis Alberts

James and Nora Ross

Nonie and Jerrold Schwartz

Cleo and James Pruden

Frances, John and Steve Wheelock

Every Sunday Abe and I read *The New York Times* and have roast beef for dinner.

Katherine and Bob Riley

It's fun to break up the glass. We're doing our thing for ecology and the Boy Scouts will give us a badge for working here.

We like to play war.

Washing cars is a great way for a group of kids to make some money.

I really love him.

There is nothing to do in Suburbia.

They're still going together.

Basically we are very much alike, the same individual. Our temperaments however are different, we reflect on things differently. My son was raised to think for himself.

My father is an ex-army officer, I'm an ex-Marine. My life-style changes were hard for my dad to understand. I'm a freer individual, not different. He doesn't understand that.

The furniture is worn out. Don and Tom have grown up and soon will leave for college. Pat will have to cook for two.

Last year I got 4 pounds of candy. 72 jelly beans, 67 Candy Corns, 26 Tootsie Rolls, 18 Tootsie Pops, 21 licorice sticks, 15 jaw breakers, 14 bubble gums, 11 packs of gum, 10 Baby Ruth bars, 11 Hershey bars, 4 Peter Paul Mounds bars, 3 Sugar Daddies, 3 popcorn balls, 3 Milky Way bars, 2 bags of cookies, 2 salt water taffy, and a candy apple. It took me three days and I ate everything.

Every year I go to my mother-in-law's for Thanksgiving and every year I swear I'll never do it again.
But I always do, do it again.

Bill Owens' family and his in-laws.

For the last four years we have given a caroling party. We sing for at least forty families in our neighborhood. We do this because we feel that Christmas has become too commercial.

We have to move. My husband's been transferred to Southern California.

Our house is built with the living room in the back, so in the evenings we sit out front of the garage and watch the traffic go by.

Fourteen years ago Dublin, California was a crossroads on U.S. 50 and Highway 21. The population was less than 1,000 (most of them cows). Today Dublin is the crossroads of Interstate Highways 580 and 680 with a population over 25,000 people. We now have fifteen gas stations, six supermarkets, two department stores, and a K-Mart. And we're still growing.

Once you hit the Freeway you can be in San Francisco in forty minutes.

DEDICATION:
This book is dedicated to Robert Harshorn Shimshak for believing in me. Without him my Suburbia negatives would still be in my basement and the prints underneath my bed. Also to my ex-wife Janet who sat at home with Andrew and Eric while I did my work, and Alfred Heller, my first supporter. Thanks to Marion Brenner and Libby McCoy who made the master prints for this book and to Bill Vandouris for invaluable technical assistance with my color work.

Bill and Janet Owens, 1970

Fotofolio
561 Broadway
New York, New York 10012

Fotofolio: Martin Bondell, Juliette Galant, Ron Schick, Cindy Williamson, Justine Keefe
Printed in Hong Kong
Library of Congress Catalog Card Number: 99-63905
ISBN: 1-881270-40-8 (hardcover)